FIGHTING BACK!

Every Woman's Guide To Survival

By   Helene Crane

Disclaimer:
The views expressed and methods recommended in this book
reflect the personal opinions of the author and are not necessarily
endorsed by any police organization.

Published by:
Beauvoir
P.O. Box 64257
5512 4 St. N.W.
Calgary, Ab. T2K 6J1

Photos by:
Carolyn Sandstrom

ISBN 0-9697160-0-1

Printed in Canada

TABLE OF CONTENTS

Acknowledgements

A number of people contributed to the writing and publishing of this book. I sincerely thank Kathryn Kopciuk and Richard Sewchuk for their wonderful and convincing poses for the demonstration photos. Also, my sister Carolyn Crane and my friend Janet Hamende for the many hours they spent editing out my mistakes. Finally, thanks to all who offered support and much needed advise: Myrna Pearman, Roseanne Hamel, Donna Prall, and of course, Faye Gowing.

I cannot name all of the people who encouraged me to complete this project. The support was overwhelming. It showed me that there was not only a need for this book, but that there is an even greater need for us to join forces and help protect each other from violence.

Dedication

This book is dedicated to the fourteen young women who were gunned down in cold blood in December, 1989 at the University of Montreal, Ecole Polythechnique (Faculty of Engineering).

INTRODUCTION

In all probability, you have decided to read this book because you are concerned with the level of violence in our society. You are worried about your safety, and the safety of those you care about. You are certainly not alone in your concern. While working as a Resource Officer in high schools and junior high schools, I received many requests for "streetproofing" presentations to students and staff. There seems to be an increasing concern for personal safety for every age group. The escalation of violent crime rates has become the single most important social issue of our times. People are realizing that they are susceptible to violent crime, and in fact, chances are they will become victims, if they have not been already.

In researching the available material for these presentations, it soon became apparent that the instructional books and tapes I was able to find were simply not good enough for my audiences. The more I searched, the more I found that these techniques the "experts" were attempting to teach were, in my opinion, either ineffective in a real life situation, or far too complex for those of us without a black belt in karate. Knowing crisis situations as I do, a person under a surprise physical attack cannot remember complicated techniques. Effective defenses must be simple, yet forceful enough to stop a vicious attacker. I have also determined, over many years as a police officer, what we can do to reduce our chances of becoming victims. Prevention is still the best defense.

In a life and death situation, a person under attack must know how to escape unharmed. All of the defenses in this book are, in my opinion, realistic methods of saving your life. While relatively simple and easy to learn, some techniques are potentially lethal to whomever is attacking you. The message you will see repeated in this book is:

DO WHATEVER IT TAKES!

If you are under attack, and you feel that your life is being threatened, you cannot hesitate. **GET HIM BEFORE HE GETS YOU!**

SURVIVAL IS ALL THAT IS IMPORTANT!

Every effort has been made to determine the most effective methods of self-defense. However, it is impossible to foresee every response to every attack, just as it is impossible to foresee every attacker's pattern. **Only you** can determine your own capabilities and evaluate a situation for a response appropriate to your skill level. The techniques discussed in this book should be practiced often and carefully with a friend. I encourage you to further build your strength and confidence levels by enrolling in a reputable self-defense course.

Chapter 1

WHAT WENT WRONG
WITH OUR WORLD?

It seems like a lifetime ago. I grew up during the "Hippie" era. There were "love children" everywhere advocating "flower power" and "make love-not war". For all its idealism and silly looking clothes, it truly was a kinder, gentler time. Today, the pendulum seems to have swung disproportionately to the other side. We are constantly bombarded with violence. In newspapers, T.V., movies, even kids' games and toys: the message is clear: "Beware, there is someone, somewhere, waiting to get you."

Violence towards women and children seems to be increasing at an alarming rate. On any given day, our newspapers tell us that children are being abducted from their own backyards, women are being attacked while jogging, and jealous men are gunning down ex-wives before turning the gun on themselves. This is no longer just a big-city problem. These events are happening in small rural communities as well as large urban centers. Our news is full of violent and inhumane examples of how our society has changed.

THE CRIME

Although women's groups have lobbied with some success to have sexual and domestic assaults, as well as child abuse dealt with more severely by law enforcement agencies and the judicial system, it appears that some people are simply not getting the message. I'm sure it comes as no great surprise to you that the incidence of violent crime has increased dramatically over the last ten years. While reports of all types of crime have increased, the most alarming increases have been in the areas of sexual assault, child abuse, domestic assault, common assault, and street robbery.

As much as I dislike statistics, I feel that it is important that you know what your risks are of being a victim of one of these crimes. The numbers show that one in four females will be the victim of some type of sexual offense by the time they reach the age of eighteen. One half of us will be sexual assault victims in our lifetimes. For males, it appears that one in ten will be the victim of similar crimes. As if these numbers aren't frightening enough, consider that they reflect only those offenses reported to police departments and sexual assault agencies. Some experts feel that for every offense reported, ten victims decide to keep the horror of what has happened to themselves, or share it only with a close friend or family member.

Victims fail to report these crimes for many valid reasons. They are numbed by shock and disbelief. They may feel somehow responsible for what happened. They may be fearful of further harm from a returning attacker. They have suffered severe psychological and physical trauma. Often the situation is complicated by the fact that the attacker is known to the victim: a boyfriend, co-worker, or family member. Any of these reasons make reporting very difficult.

WHO IS THE ENEMY?

The reasons why someone would threaten to attack you are very limited. They may be thieves, wanting only your property. In this case, if you feel they are capable of harming you, you should turn over what they want. Possessions are simply not worth getting injured or killed over.

The other motivation for an attack is because they wish to cause you physical harm. The kind of confrontation we all fear the most is one by a psychotic killer and/or rapist. Most are planned in advance, although the attacker may not have selected a specific target. Why men rape is a puzzle the "experts" have yet to solve. First, I must clarify the terms. Rape is a word we all immediately recognize and fear. The word, however, only refers to the act of forced intercourse. Many other sexual acts are often forced upon the victim, none of which are any less horrifying to her. Sexual assault is the legal term now used to describe any forced assault of a sexual nature. When I refer to either rape or sexual assault, I refer to any and all of these acts. We are talking about crimes primarily of violence, not sex. It is simply the use of power over another human being.

Sexual assault is most often committed by someone the victim knows. In fact, experts believe that this type of assault accounts for over 75% of all attacks on women. The attacker can be an acquaintance, boyfriend, family member, co-worker, or even a husband. While victims in these circumstances suffer the same kinds of short and long term trauma as those attacked by strangers, these crimes are the least likely to be reported. Attackers in these cases are no less criminals than the strangers lurking in the bushes waiting for an unsuspecting victim to happen by.

Surveys of women in universities and colleges reveal frightening results. At least 25% report they have been sexually assaulted by boyfriends or acquaintances; a "date rape" situation. Most do not report these incidents. Male students, and remarkably, a majority of female students cite that this type of abuse is an indicator of love, and that the violence reflected jealousy, a response to sexual denial, or simply drinking too much. Try to imagine how these numbers would explode if spousal attacks were included.

Although statistically a rare occurrence, what scares us the most is being attacked by a stranger. For any woman walking alone, and facing a suspicious-looking male on the sidewalk, statistics alone are not too reassuring. This is the situation we fear the most; what we have been taught to be terrified of. This is the dreaded "stranger attack" by a cold-blooded "rapist".

Rapists are angry. They seek power and control over women and/or children. They DO NOT have uncontrollable sexual urges! They enjoy degrading and humiliating their victims. Helped by a society filled with pornography and violence, they have learned to treat women with contempt, merely objects to conquer and upon whom to vent their anger. Unfortunately, there is no universal pattern as to what makes a rapist or murderer. Each situation, and each attacker is different. Some are scared off when a woman resists or fights back. Others get more excited by the challenge of resistance. All of them enjoy seeing the fear and panic in the victim's eyes. One thing is known, they seek out those who appear vulnerable. They don't look for someone who will give them a good, fair fight!

It is impossible to tell you one perfect response to every attacker. In the past, police agencies recommended to women that if they were attacked, the best thing for them to do was submit to their attacker, in order to avoid injury. The only problem was that the victim then had to explain to investigators and courtrooms why, if she hadn't consented to the act, she had no bruises or visible signs of attack. Surprisingly, recent studies have shown that women who **do fight back** get away more often than those who remain passive! Also, the more defense strategies a woman uses- yelling, kicking, pleading, running, biting, scratching, the more likely she is to escape serious injury.

THE REAL POLICE STORY

When I became a police officer, it was a tremendous cultural shock to me. I was a middle class, idealistic young optimist. I thought I had lots of friends, and the world was a wonderful place. Then, I put on a blue uniform, and suddenly the world wasn't so beautiful, and a lot of my "friends" stopped calling. At social gatherings, people would act differently around me and watch what they said. Or worse, they would proceed to complain to me about how they were treated by the traffic cop who caught them speeding last week. But those are the hazards of the profession. I chose this career because I believed I could help people, and somehow make a difference to our world. In fact, if all of the police officers in Canada and the United States were asked why they chose law enforcement as a career, you would find the vast majority simply want to help people and contribute to making our society a better place. It certainly isn't for the huge salaries and wonderful working conditions. We all want to catch the bad guys and save the innocent victims of the world. Disillusionment comes quickly as we realize that we only catch a fraction of the bad guys. When we do catch one, he often walks out the front door of the police station while we're still typing the reports. Or worse, he walks from court because of a legal technicality. Try explaining that to your victim, who has recounted her horror story for the twentieth time on the witness stand.

I believe that each one of us is here on this earth for a purpose. We have a reason for being, and I believe my reason for being here is to help those who are targets of violent crimes. Over the years, I have investigated attacks on many women, children, seniors, and even the handicapped. While it is extremely difficult not to get emotionally involved, it is absolutely essential to maintain our professionalism during an investigation. When we lose our objectivity, we run the risk of tainting evidence, thus enabling the bad guy to "walk". Try to imagine how difficult it is to maintain your objectivity when interviewing someone you suspect has just sexually assaulted a six year old girl. She is hospitalized with physical injuries, not to mention the psychological trauma that will be with her for the rest of her life. You must treat this suspect with respect, and offer him all of the comforts available, as well as a lawyer. And don't forget to read him his rights!

Sadly, the future does not look any better. In fact, indications are that crime rates will continue to climb. Law enforcement agencies do not have the budgets to hire the numbers of officers it would take to protect us all. We had better learn to take care of ourselves, or at least, join with other community resources to help keep our neighborhoods safe. If you dislike feeling vulnerable, and are tired of being afraid to go out alone, you must learn how to take care of yourself. TAKE RESPONSIBILITY FOR YOUR OWN PERSONAL SAFETY.

THE POWER OF ATTITUDE

Thanks to the Women's Movement, all of us are learning to be more independent, confident, and strong. Society's passion for physical fitness has contributed to all of these attributes as well. Unfortunately, many women were brought up to be quiet, submissive, polite, and accommodating. It is foreign to them to act aggressively and physically. Unlike little boys, many of us were not encouraged to be competitive and fight for our territory. Whereas boys are taught to be physical and aggressive through football, wrestling, and countless other contact sports, most girls are encouraged to play with dolls and learn how to cook.

Being assertive is very unnatural to most of us, but it is a tremendous defense, as attackers are not prepared for an aggressive victim. They are looking for the weak and meek.

We have already established the fact that resisting attack works. Now, all you have to do is develop the confidence that will enable you to become angry enough to actually injure your attacker. While this may sound like an obvious reaction, given that you will naturally be angry if confronted, there is a vast difference between being angry, and being angry enough to do significant physical damage to another human being. The term "seeing red" is the degree of anger you may need to defend yourself. This is the "you or me" mind set. It is very difficult for most of us to reach this level of anger. In fact, I would hazard a guess that most of us have only reached that state once or twice in our lifetimes. What would it take to make you "see red"? Someone attacking your child? One of your family? How would your loved ones feel if you were injured or killed? Is this enough to get you REALLY ANGRY? Think about their reaction to seeing you lying in a hospital bed.

The problem is, you never know how you are going to react to a physical threat until the situation arises. My first experiences as a police officer were extremely disturbing. These were situations with violent, drug or alcohol-induced "crazies", who were out of control. I have relived many of these fights in my dreams for years afterwards. Once the adrenaline stops flowing through your veins, you can regain some control. Adrenaline is nature's way of supplying us with incredible strength and pain suppressant. Unfortunately, the attacker is usually having an adrenaline rush as well. The difference is that a police officer is trying only to subdue and arrest this person. As a possible victim, you may have to injure and disable him, at least long enough to make your escape.

If you are ever faced with this type of situation, try to remember that **YOU MUST GET HIM BEFORE HE GETS YOU!** You did not create this situation- **HE DID!** You are a very valuable person to a lot of loved ones, and your welfare is all that is important. What happens to him is insignificant. Anger will get the adrenaline moving, and give you the extra strength and faster reaction time you need to have the edge over him. Panic will only cause you to freeze and become helpless. You must be prepared to do real physical damage to this person. **You must do whatever it takes to prevent being a victim.**

I remember being called to attend a hospital where a prostitute was reporting a serious sexual assault. She was lying in her hospital bed with black eyes, swollen face, cuts, and contusions. She reported that she had been attacked by a "john", for no apparent reason. He had simply picked up a large rock on the floor of his pick-up truck, and began bashing in her skull! As he was beating her into unconsciousness, she gathered the strength and courage to shove her thumb deep into her attacker's eye. While he was preoccupied with this excruciating pain, our victim managed to make her escape. My job was to wait for someone with an eye injury trying to obtain medical attention at a hospital in our vicinity. Fortunately, our victim had done enough damage to require our "bad guy" to plead for help, and we were happy to respond to another hospital's report of an incoming patient requiring help with his damaged eye!

The moral of this story is to DO WHATEVER IT TAKES! You must use your gut instincts to determine whether this situation requires your fiercest reaction. Be aware of your identity, "I am a special human being, valued by many loved ones, and ready to do battle with anyone wanting to take my basic human rights away from me." There is no such thing as a "FAIR FIGHT" in these situations. **ANYTHING GOES**: you must do whatever it takes to preserve your well- being.

LEGAL RIGHTS AND RESPONSIBILITIES

It always amazes me how many people are preoccupied with the threat of being sued. Under all laws in modern civilized societies, we are allowed to use **reasonable force** to prevent being attacked, or act in self-defense. We may use as much force as is necessary to stop the attack upon us. In other words, a simple verbal threat may not be reason enough to physically attack whomever is threatening you. However, once you are **convinced** this person is going to attack you, use as much force as is necessary to stop the attack. Worrying about a possible criminal charge or lawsuit against you should be the last thing on your mind. If you feel your life is in danger, DO WHATEVER IT TAKES.

Sometimes, in the heat of the moment, with adrenaline flowing, a victim may be so blinded by anger that she does not realize how much damage she is inflicting. The important thing to remember is that once you are satisfied your attacker cannot continue the attack, however temporarily, MAKE YOUR GET-AWAY. Even though your anger level is at its highest, your objective should not be to inflict more injury on this individual. The objective is to disable him sufficiently to allow you to escape unharmed.

TRUST YOUR INSTINCTS and believe in your worth and value as a human being. Worry about being sued after you are safe and sound, surrounded by those who care about you!

Chapter 2

STAYING SAFE

I have spoken with women who are accomplished martial arts competitors and instructors. When asked what they would do if physically attacked by a 200 lb. male, they invariably reply, "I would run like hell". In 1983, Lisa Sliwa, National Director of the Guardian Angels citizen protection group, was attacked by three men. They had knocked her almost unconscious in preparing to rape her, and the last effort she could summon was to yell as loud as she could, and grab one of her attackers in the crotch. This was enough to scare the gang off. Although she has a black belt in karate, she was no match for this fight. What saved her was her attitude that nobody was going to rape her. She would fight to the end. What Sliwa preaches now is that women must learn to be "streetwise". In other words, the best way to prevent being a target, is to be vigilant, and have a plan.

In a perfect world, we would be unafraid to walk, cycle, or jog wherever and whenever we wanted. We would invite someone over for a sociable drink, or even, if the urge struck us, walk down the street with no clothes on without fear of being attacked. Unfortunately, as we all know, any of these actions carry a strong risk factor with them. The world being as it is, we only have to look at which businesses are thriving today. The fastest growing enterprises supply and sell security devices: home and car alarm systems, self-defense weapons, private security personnel, special door locks and devices, window bars, etc. The focus is on PREVENTION. We want to make it difficult for the bad guys to pick us as a target. If we can slow them down, or deter them, they will hopefully move on to an easier target.

Let's look at some common, everyday situations we all experience. If you had not thought about these as potentially dangerous, perhaps you should take particular note. My experience with most victims is that they had no idea that where they were or what they were doing was making them a target. Being vigilant does not mean being paranoid. Fear of attack does not have to take over your life. Some simple precautions, practiced everyday, become second-nature. You will learn to drive with your doors locked, just as you have (hopefully) learned to use your seatbelts at all times

WALKING ALONE

Remember always that attackers are not looking for resistance or a "fair fight". They seek out targets who appear weak, easily intimidated, and possibly, already fearful. The most important image to project on a street is one of a strong, confident person. This is best done by walking assertively, with straight posture, unafraid to look someone in the eye. This does not mean staring offensively at someone coming towards you, as this might actually provoke a confrontation. It simply means looking at someone long enough to be able to describe him, if need be. You might be surprised at how many people cannot describe their attackers at all, simply because they walk with their eyes down almost all of the time.

Common sense precautions to take when walking alone include staying in well lit areas at night. Do not take shortcuts through parks, alleys, or schoolyards, even though it might get you to your destination quicker. Stay where there are people. Walk facing oncoming traffic so that a vehicle cannot sneak up on you from behind. For a vehicle to follow you while you face oncoming traffic, the driver would have to drive in reverse.

If you think you may have someone following you on foot, get to where there are people: a convenience store, gas station, or firehall. TRUST YOUR INSTINCTS. If you have a bad feeling about someone walking behind you, and you fear the gap between you is closing, run as fast as you can to a safe place. Don't worry about feeling foolish or mistaking a respectable citizen for a stalker. It is not worth the risk. Far better you look a little silly running down the street than take the chance that your instincts are wrong. Trust yourself. The worst possible situation is to be grabbed from behind. This catches you off guard and off balance. The advantage of the element of surprise is totally with the attacker.

If the gap has closed and your instincts tell you that this person is after you, **YOU MUST CONFRONT HIM.** This means turning around and assuming a defensive stance (see photo, chapter 3). In a very **LOUD and AGGRESSIVE** voice, say "What the hell do you want from me?", or "Quit following me!" This reverses the element of surprise and will, hopefully, attract the attention of anyone nearby. The attacker is definitely not ready for this aggressive reaction. He was expecting a cowering, quivering, defenseless target. The most important point is not to wait until this person is close enough to grab you from behind. You must act first in order to get the upper hand. **TURN AND FACE HIM!** Don't worry about looking foolish. You can always apologize to an innocent person. This is far preferable to risking being jumped from behind. **DO NOT WAIT! TRUST YOUR INSTINCTS!**

The person following you may be a thief, in which case you should not put up a fight. Your possessions are simply not worth getting injured or killed over. One case which always comes to mind involved an elderly woman waiting at a bus stop. Two young males came by and grabbed for her purse. Rather than give in to her attackers, this brave woman hung on tight to her purse straps. She was not going to give it up without a fight. They knocked her to the ground and dragged her by her purse straps down the sidewalk until the straps broke, and the thugs ran off with her purse. I took this report from the hospital, where our victim was being treated for multiple contusions, bruising, and a dislocated shoulder. All that was in her purse was $20 cash, identification, and a set of keys. The cash was minimal, the identification replaceable, and her door locks easily re-keyed. These items were not worth the physical damage done to her. Possessions are meaningless when compared to your physical well-being.

An excellent escape technique to use in a "mugging" situation is, when the thief demands your money, take it out of your purse or pocket and throw it on the ground far away from you. While the thief looks and reaches for the money, run away as fast as you can. He will choose to stay and gather up the money, unless it wasn't just money he was after.

If the person following you is not a thief, but is out to do you serious harm, you have faced and confronted him first. This gives you the advantage of surprise, and it just might be enough to make him change his mind. Remember the discussion on who these attackers are? Studies have shown that many attackers are actually scared off by women who are not afraid to fight. For those who aren't scared off, at least you are facing your assailant and are in your defensive stance, ready to use the techniques to be discussed in the next chapter.

AT HOME

Nowhere should we feel safer than in our own homes. It is our safe haven, our sanctuary, our cocoon. We never expect to be targets in our own home, but, as we discussed earlier, most often women and children are attacked by someone they know, and often in their own home. We need to make our homes as secure as possible, without making it feel like a prison.

Call your local police department to see if they will conduct a home security check. Often, they will make recommendations that are relatively easy and inexpensive. Basic home security should include good deadbolt locks on all exterior doors, metal bars and pins to eliminate horizontal and vertical movement on all sliding glass doors and windows, and bars on basement windows.

An alarm system is expensive, but effective, especially if it sounds a pre-entry alarm. This would alert your neighbors that there is a problem at your house even before a housebreaker actually enters. Some alarms are monitored by security companies, who then contact the police if the system is activated. The problem with alarms is the human error involved. Home owners, their children, and even their pets often accidentally set off their alarm systems. Once there have been several false alarms, police stop responding and complacency sets in. It is very similar to car alarms going off in parking lots. Have you noticed how no one even turns to look in the direction of car alarms anymore? You may want to consider something as simple as buying a "Beware of Dog" sign and very large dog dish for the backyard. Much cheaper than an alarm system, but very effective as a deterrent.

Good exterior lighting is important too. Dark shrubbery makes excellent hiding places. Motion detector lights are a great idea. If someone steps into range, they turn on immediately to warn you of an intruder.

Everyone in your home should be instructed in the proper way to answer the door and telephone. Never open the door to someone you do not know. I know it may sound rude, but people can hear perfectly well through a closed door. Ask who they are and what they want. Identification is carried by anyone who would legitimately need to enter your home on business. If they do not provide it, DO NOT OPEN THE DOOR! A common story is the distressed motorist who needs to use your phone. Tell him you will call whomever he wants while he waits outside your LOCKED door.

Similarly, telephone etiquette states that we shall be polite to everyone. We surrender far too much information over the phone. How many times have you given out your credit card number to someone over the phone? We tell poll-takers if we are married, how many people live in our house, how much money we make, and on and on. What if the poll-taker is really not a poll-taker at all? Do not give out personal information on the telephone.

Obscene calls should invoke no response other than hanging up. These callers want a reaction from you. They want you to be upset. Do not use a whistle to damage the caller's ear drum. He could call back and do the same to you or someone in your family. Obscene and threatening phone calls are against the law. Record the dates and times of each, and call your telephone company. Most companies have the equipment to instantly identify the phone number of the caller. If the problem persists, the best solution may be getting an unlisted number.

IN YOUR CAR

Someone close to me was once driving home very late at night. There was hardly any traffic on the road. As she pulled up behind another car at a red light, the male driver of the car in front got out and ran toward her. She managed to push the door lock down just as he reached for the handle. He then jumped on the hood of her car and began to pound on the windshield. She couldn't go forward, so she put the car into reverse and stepped on the gas. Luckily, there was nothing in the way! She slammed on the brakes and cranked the wheel, and the crazed attacker went flying! If this doesn't convince you to drive with your doors locked at all times, I don't know what will. Carjacking may be the crime of the future, so we will need to be extra vigilant while driving.

If you think you are being followed in your car, **DO NOT** try to lose them or outrun them. This will most likely result in an accident. Try honking your horn repeatedly, to attract attention. Drive to where there are people: a convenience store, gas station, fire hall, or police station. Getting a licence plate number is very helpful, but not as important as getting to help.

Park in well-lit areas, and avoid dark parkades. Always have your keys ready and check the back seat before getting in. Cellular phones are excellent security if your car breaks down or you think you are being followed. Just seeing you speak into a phone is usually enough to scare off someone who is following you, especially if you are looking into your rearview mirror, reciting his licence number.

If your car breaks down, especially at night, stay inside with your hazard lights flashing and doors locked. When someone stops to help, open your window, just a crack, and ask them to phone for a tow truck or the police.

One final note about vehicles. Never, ever, allow yourself to be coerced into a vehicle. Statistics show that a person's chances of survival drop dramatically if they are taken to a secondary location. Use every physical defense you can muster to prevent being taken away in a vehicle.

AT WORK

In addition to our homes, most of us feel safe and secure in our workplace. We don't expect to be attacked in familiar surroundings. However, in places where the public has access, or is invited to enter, the risk is always there that someone dangerous may be lurking close by.

Places to be on the alert include bathrooms, elevators, secluded storage rooms, and anywhere that puts you at a distance from work colleagues. Have you ever been waiting for an elevator, and when the doors open, there is only one person inside, and he gives you an instant uneasy feeling? Well, you are not alone. We have all felt this way. The astonishing thing is, WE GET IN ANYWAY! We will go against all of our instincts and good judgement simply because we feel obliged to get in that elevator. Why not walk away, or state that you are waiting for an elevator going in the other direction? Or, if you are already on the elevator and others are preparing to leave you alone with someone you don't trust: why not leave with them? So what if it's not your floor. Catch another elevator! If you determine that something is about to happen and you cannot get off the elevator in time, push the ALARM button (not the STOP button), and all of the floor buttons. This will alert others that there may be a serious problem on this elevator.

People who work evening and night shifts are often at risk when going to their cars. Parking lots and parkades are becoming common crime scenes. Many hospitals have implemented an escort system for nurses going to their cars after dark. Other organizations have started a telephone system cars after dark. Other organizations have started a telephone system whereby the employee calls back to work once they have arrived safely home. This type of "buddy" system is an excellent back-up to personal safety.

More and more we hear about sexual harassment in the workplace. Prominent business executives, politicians, and even judges are being successfully prosecuted and sued for such conduct. But most disturbing is the fact that almost all of us have, at some time, been sexually harassed in the workplace. For those of us in traditionally male professions, this can be in the form of put-downs, sexually explicit jokes, or being denied certain positions. Other types of sexual harassment may be in the form of requests for sexual favours in return for job security or advancement. Whatever the form or reason for such treatment, it is illegal, and potentially dangerous. A sexually aggressive co-worker can present as frightening a confrontation as a complete stranger can. The fact that you know the attacker may make you hesitant to yell or use physical force against him. He knows this. This is much like a "date rape" situation. He may also be your immediate supervisor, using that form of power over you. He may challenge you by saying it is all a test to see if you "can take it".

My recommendation to anyone being harassed at work is to first confront the person making the unwanted comments or actions. You must make it absolutely clear that his advances or crude behavior are not welcome. Document all dates, times, conversations, and actions. If one warning is not enough to stop this unwanted behavior, go to the next supervisory level within the company or organization. If no action is taken, go to the next level, in addition to a representative from your union or employee group. If you have no employee organization, talk to other women at work. Chances are, you are not the first one to be harassed by this individual. Or, it may be revealed that there are other offenders within the organization. By coming forward together, victims are not as reluctant to report incidents. The worst thing to do is nothing. By doing nothing you are condoning such behavior and actually encouraging the offenders to continue with you and your co-workers.

There have been many reports of women being fired for pursuing complaints of sexual harassment. If this were the case, I would encourage them to go to local women's groups for support, and write letters to the media. It is amazing how these companies will finally "do the right thing", once these stories become public.

Chapter 3

FIGHTING BACK

In Chapter 2 we discussed how to minimize your chance of becoming a target of violent crime. Unfortunately, as with much in life, there are no guarantees. People are attacked in broad daylight, with plenty of potential helpers and witnesses close by. Even in a mall parking lot, at one o'clock in the afternoon, you must be vigilant and trust your instincts. One thing I often hear from victims is, "I felt funny about this guy from the first moment I saw him". Your gut feelings are usually correct. The best self- defense is **awareness and escape.**

At the point you determine that you are about to be physically confronted, and that you cannot escape, you must decide on how you will defend yourself. In some cases, such as when the attacker is using a deadly weapon, you may decide that fighting back would mean certain death or serious injury. Many women have survived weapon attacks using "passive defenses", which will be discussed in greater detail in Chapter 4. In short, passive defenses require women to become great actresses, pretending to submit to their attacker. This technique may calm him down to the point where he lets down his guard, and the woman can make her get away.

PHYSICAL DEFENSES

You do not need a black belt in karate to successfully defend yourself or your loved ones. In fact, as stated earlier, some women who have studied martial arts have experienced a total blank when attacked. The panic and terror that rushed over them caused their memories to completely shut down. They were immobilized with panic. That is why I believe in teaching only a few basic (but extremely effective) techniques. It is the old K.I.S.S. Principle (keep it simple stupid). If you **practice, practice, practice** these few points, you should be able to react, almost instinctively, under stress.

Mental practice is just as important as physical practice. Role-playing with a friend, making faces and yelling at a mirror, and picturing yourself in highly stressful situations, will all contribute to your mental preparedness. In the following physical defenses, we will emphasize the importance of using **SURPRISE, SPEED, AND AGGRESSION.** Try acting a defense out in front of a mirror, or see how well it works when role-playing with someone else. Most women are extremely reluctant to hurt anyone, even when under attack, but try to remember: **IF YOU THINK SOMEONE IS OUT TO HARM YOU, YOU MUST HURT HIM BEFORE HE HURTS YOU!**

Fighting Stance- front view

CONTROLLING FEAR

Fear is a natural reaction to confrontation, but, if fear leads to panic and "freezing", it can prevent you from protecting yourself. If you cover your face and recoil into a sobbing mess, you will surely lose. By turning your fear into anger, you begin the flow of adrenalin. Adrenalin produces the "fight or flight" syndrome, which is nature's way of empowering us when we are threatened. Vision and hearing become more acute, strength increases dramatically, reaction times are quicker, and our pain threshold increases. To gain the benefits of this adrenalin rush, fear must be turned into anger, not panic. Here are some basic steps designed to achieve that result:

1. BREATHE- Holding your breath is a sure fire way to " freeze". When you are shocked by something, you tend to sharply inhale and hold your breath. If confronted, you must consciously make yourself exhale and breathe deeply. Think about it: oxygen keeps the brain alert, muscles ready to react, and keeps you calm. Remember what you were always told about public speaking? "Take a few deep breaths to relax". The same holds true for confrontations. Breathing will help to keep you calm and in control, even giving you a sense of power. Breathe deeply and steadily. **Do not hold your breath!**

2. STRONG BODY LANGUAGE-Once you are convinced someone is out to harm you, you must confront them. You should turn to face them and state (in a loud and aggressive voice), "What the hell do you want?" or "Quit following me!". You must also protect your personal space. I recommend that you let them get no closer to you than four paces. Anything less than that puts you within grabbing range. Equally important is to avoid being grabbed from the rear. It is much more difficult to defend yourself when attacked from behind. **Turn and face him!**

Next, assume the fighting stance shown opposite. Feet are approximately shoulder width apart, with one foot slightly ahead of the other. Knees are flexed and weight is on the balls of the feet. Hands are poised for blocking and striking. This stance makes you look like you know martial arts, and may be enough to make your attacker have second thoughts. It also gives you a strong, balanced position, from which all other moves will originate. Being in this balanced position makes it more difficult for someone to drag you down to the ground (the last place you want to be in a fight). It also establishes your zone of personal space. You are, in effect, saying "Don't come any closer or you will be very, very sorry !" Just assuming this stance should make you feel more confident and strong. Try it! Yes, right now! How does it make you feel ?

Fighting Stance- side view

3. YELL/ MAKE NOISE- Don't worry about causing a scene. While high-pitched screams sound scared, a deep guttural roar sounds strong and angry. Everything you yell must be negative; "NO..NO..NO!", or "Stay away from me or I'll kill you!" One convicted child serial killer was asked by a reporter if any children ever got away from him, and he stated that he would leave alone the ones who yelled "NO" the loudest and most persistently. Attackers do not want to draw attention to themselves. They prey on society's obsession with never creating a scene. The newspapers often report foiled bank robberies where, when handed the hold-up note, the teller speaks up and says "NO, you're not getting my money!". The would-be robbers are last seen running out of the bank empty- handed!

Besides yelling to draw attention, deep abdominal roars focus strength. As in martial arts, a loud yell always accompanies a critical kick or blow. Not only does it focus your blow, it also serves as a distraction to shock or scare the opponent. Practice yelling in front of a mirror. You must get used to hearing these sounds or you may even scare yourself.

WHERE TO TAKE AIM

By now, I hope you have decided that if attacked, you will do **WHATEVER IT TAKES!** You will bite, kick, knee, punch, gouge, rip, or any combination of these. Each of these techniques has been successful, at one time or another. Unfortunately using these defenses can be a total waste of your energy if the attacker is hit where there is little feeling. You want to strike where there are lots of nerves and very little cushioning fat or muscle. These are called pressure or trigger points. To punch or pound on a man's chest or shoulders is a complete waste of your valuable strength. In order to make your strikes count, you must aim for the most sensitive areas on his body.

The first area we think of striking is the groin. While it is definitely a highly sensitive area, it is also the most easily protected part of a man's body. It is the first place he will reach to protect. Since he was a small child, barely able to walk, he was taught to protect his genitals. Men are very adept at quickly avoiding injuries there. They also expect this to be your target. If you look carefully at the following diagram, you will see that the groin is a very specific target. There are no other trigger points close by. If you miss or only partially make contact, your attacker will not only be uninjured, he will become even more angry and violent toward you.

Look at some of the other pressure points. Note how many are clustered around the head and face. Virtually any blow which makes contact with the face is going to cause extreme pain. If you have ever been slapped across the face, you will definitely remember how it felt, and how long the pain and stinging remained. The face is also an area we all automatically move quickly to protect from blows. If you plan on striking someone in the face, it had better be done with such speed and power that your target will not have a chance to block you. Memorize these trigger points. As we move through the techniques, we will refer to these points.

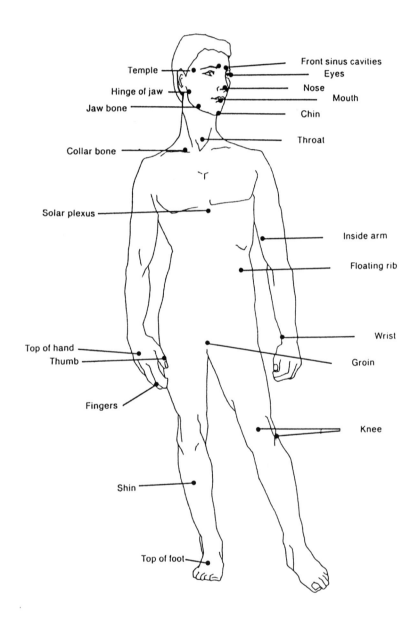

DEFENDING AGAINST FRONTAL ATTACKS

From this point on, we will assume that you are defending yourself against an all-out violent attack. Once you have decided to use physical defenses, there is no turning back. The most important thing to remember is: if you decide to fight, you must be **TOTALLY COMMITTED** to seriously injure your attacker. This might sound obvious, but I have seen too many victims who changed their minds too late. You cannot strike a half-hearted blow, then decide to try **talking** your attacker out of it. Passive defenses should be attempted at the beginning of a confrontation. If you sense that this is not working, and you are going to be attacked, **YOU MUST STRIKE FIRST, WITH TOTAL COMMITMENT TO SERIOUSLY INJURE HIM.**

If you are having trouble picturing yourself reacting this angrily and aggressively, it is very doubtful you would have the total commitment needed to injure an attacker. Perhaps you should concentrate more on the passive defenses. Many women have difficulty remembering:

YOU DID NOT START THIS FIGHT- HE DID !

I cannot overemphasize the importance of striking the first blow. You cannot wait for your attacker to make the first move. If he hits you or grabs you first, you will likely not get another chance. Women cannot fight fairly with men. Men are simply bigger and stronger than us. The only chance you have is to catch him off guard and strike an effective blow before he touches you. This must be done as soon as he moves into your personal space. If he moves in, there should be no question in your mind that he is going to attack. **YOU MUST ATTACK FIRST!**

The following techniques deal with attacks from the front. You have turned to face your attacker, have assumed your fighting stance, confronted him verbally, and are **BREATHING** steadily.

GO FOR THE THROAT

Once he moves inside your personal "zone", you must act with **SURPRISE, SPEED, AND AGGRESSION.** We discussed earlier how critical it is to keep breathing. Panic sets in when oxygen stops flowing. We use this same principle on him, as our main defense. Your first target should be your attacker's windpipe. By **hitting** his throat with the "V" of your hand, grab his windpipe (thumb on one side, fingers on the other), and **squeeze very tightly.** You will completely cut off his oxygen supply. Make no mistake here. This is not simply a reach and grab motion. Your hand must strike his throat, just like throwing a punch. He will panic and grab at your arm to pull it away. You must hang on tightly, squeezing until his oxygen runs out. If he manages to get your hand off of his throat, he will likely need to gasp for air for a second or two; just long enough for you to break loose and run to safety.

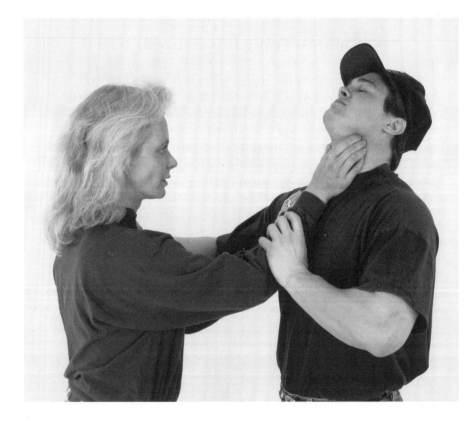

Throat Grab

EYE GOUGE

We know that the face is the most sensitive part of the body. The next few defenses will deal with various targets on the face. Many victims I know have escaped from their attackers by damaging their eyes, either by jamming their thumbs, or raking all of their fingers into his eyes. These techniques can cause severe and permanent damage. When eyes are hurt, it completely immobilizes a person. All they can do is cover their eyes with their hands. Their sight is lost for a period of time, and so they are disoriented and helpless. A perfect opportunity for escape!

Eye Gouge

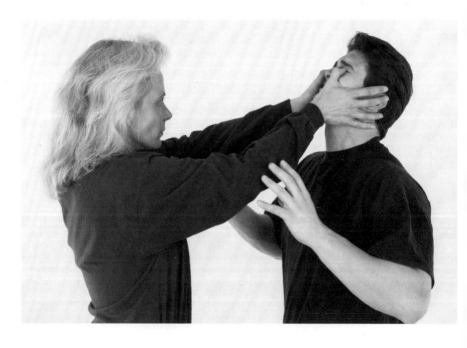

Eye Gouge- Using Thumbs

THE NOSE

The nose is made up mostly of cartilage, skin, and nerve endings. Approximately half way up the nose begins the bony protrusion. This bone is relatively fine and easily broken.

This next technique is one of the most deadly. It involves striking the heel of your hand against the end of the nose, and driving the bone up toward the top of the skull. Try to remember: THIS IS NOT A FAIR FIGHT. YOU MUST DO WHATEVER IS NECESSARY!

In a life and death situation, this technique must be done with true conviction. It cannot be a warning blow. There will be no second chance. TOTAL COMMITMENT is necessary to end this confrontation! Look carefully at the demonstration photo below.

Heel of Hand To Nose

Another method of stopping an attacker involves striking down with the side of your fist onto the top of your attacker's nose. If executed properly, this should cause enough pain to stop him in his tracks. A great deal of force can be exerted when striking downward like this, if the opportunity to strike the target is there. Again, this cannot be effective if the blow is half-hearted: **TOTAL COMMITMENT**.

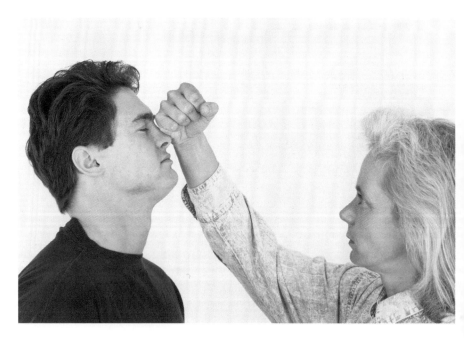

Fist Down on Nose

If the attacker has your arms and hands pinned down, you may still be able to break his hold by striking his face or nose with your forehead. You will likely not have much room to gain momentum, so the head butt will have to be very forceful and well placed to be effective.

Head Butt to Nose

THE GROIN

We have discussed how difficult it can be to strike an effective blow to the groin area. Men are very adept at turning quickly or covering this target. Usually, the kick or knee is slightly off target, rendering it ineffective. All that is accomplished is a heightened level of anger toward the victim. Kicks are most often deflected, or worse, the woman's foot is grabbed, and she is knocked off balance to the ground.

However, if the target is open, and there is a good chance of hitting it effectively, the attacker can certainly be disabled at least long enough for your escape. For example, if he has his hands on your throat, or he is holding your arms, he cannot quickly cover his groin for protection. In effect, he is "leaving himself wide open". If your hands are free, **drive** a punch directly into his groin. Punch as if you want your fist to go right through his body. If he has your arms pinned, use your knee. Drive your knee up and through to his head.

Fist To Groin

DEFENDING AGAINST ATTACKS FROM THE REAR

One of the reasons I have stressed the importance of turning to face someone who is following you, is because of the extreme disadvantage you have when being grabbed from behind. The person following you chooses when and how to attack. He has the advantage of the element of surprise. You don't have the opportunity to attempt any passive defenses, let alone prepare yourself mentally for the anger level you will need. There are fewer effective physical defenses available to you, but, there are still many ways to win.

THE CHOKE HOLD

A common rear attack involves a choke hold, where the attacker wraps his arm around your throat, thus cutting off your oxygen supply. If the front of your throat gets into the crook of his elbow, he needs only squeeze his biceps, and the blood supply in your carotid artery is cut off! Unable to breathe and with no blood reaching the brain, you may become unconscious within seconds, or dead within minutes! This is a fairly common arrest control technique used by police officers in life and death situations. It is used to "subdue" very violent suspects, and it is extremely effective. Occasionally the hold is left on too long and the suspect looses consciousness, or even dies. This can happen, quite literally, within minutes.

If this hold is ever put on you, you must break away immediately. Once the attacker is able to squeeze shut the arteries which run up the side of your neck, you will probably not be able to defend yourself. The pictures on the following pages show you how to prevent this from happening.

When you feel someone's arm wrapping around your neck, get your hands between his arm and your neck. By pushing away, you will prevent him from closing around your throat and the carotid artery. Turn towards him and **GO FOR HIS THROAT! Grab and squeeze with all your might, and do not let go.** He will have to release his choke hold on you. You can break and run while he is gasping for air.

Practice this defense with a friend. Be very careful though. If the blood supply to the brain is cut off, even for a few seconds, you could cause someone to pass out. The choke hold is extremely dangerous. There must be no kidding around when practicing this defense. Note how it feels when your throat is grabbed as well when a rear choke hold is applied to you. When the oxygen is cut off, the need to release the pressure is the only thing you can think of. This is why you must cut off your attacker's oxygen before he cuts off your's. It is one of the very few methods to release a choke hold.

Rear Choke Hold- note hand placement

Throat Grab- break and run

HEAD BUTT

As we discussed earlier, the face is an excellent target for our defensive moves. In a rear attack, especially when your arms are pinned, you can drive your head back into your attacker's face. Unless there is a great height difference, you are assured of striking a sensitive area. This should cause him to release his grip on you at least long enough for you to escape.

Rear Head Butt

FOOT STOMP

An effective defense against a rear attack is the simple, but powerful, foot stomp. The foot is made up of many small, fine bones. A well placed stomp, especially with hard-soled or high-heeled shoes, will probably break one or more of these bones. Remember, the stomp must be forceful and well placed, using your heel as the driving force.

A variation of this move is to drag your heel down the attacker's shin, in a scraping motion. This will cause extreme pain. Either of these maneuvers works well on rear attacks.

Foot Stomp

THE GROIN

Often, an attack from the rear involves the victim being placed in a headlock or strangle hold. The following photos show how the attacker can leave himself wide open to either elbows or fists to his groin. If there is a clear shot, and his hands are occupied elsewhere, USE THE OPPORTUNITY! But don't miss, and make sure there is enough force to stop him in his tracks.

Headlock- Fist to Groin

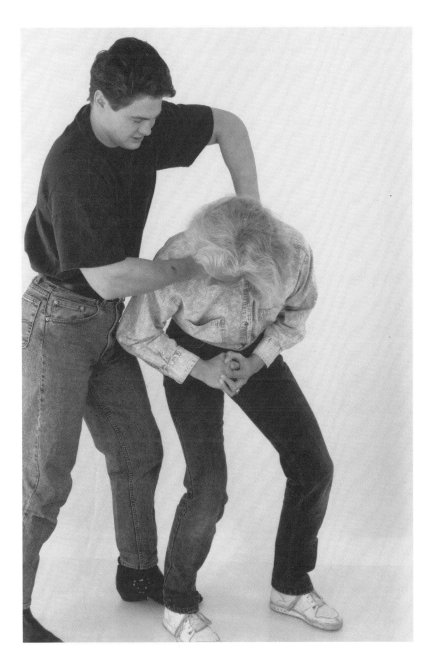

Strangle Hold- Elbow to Groin

FINGER PULLS

Often forgotten pressure points are the fingers. By pulling back on the fingers and thumbs, you can force someone to release their grip on you. Remember this if someone grabs any part of your body, particularly your neck. Try this on a partner, but remember, be very careful not to pull too far!

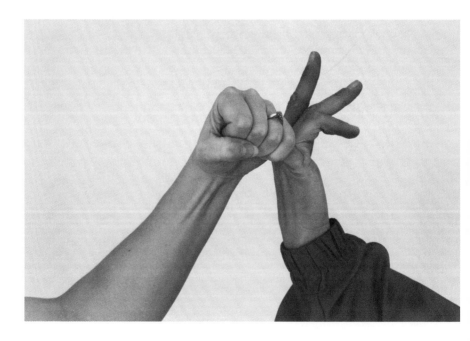

Finger Pulls

KEY POINTS TO REMEMBER

* AWARENESS AND ESCAPE ARE THE BEST DEFENSES

* HAVE A PLAN

* TRUST YOUR INSTINCTS

* ONLY YOU CAN DECIDE WHAT TYPE OF DEFENSE IS BEST FOR YOU

* PRACTICE, PRACTICE, PRACTICE

PHYSICAL DEFENSES

* GET ANGRY

* ATTACK FIRST

* USE SURPRISE, SPEED, AND AGGRESSION

* FIGHT TO WIN-DON'T FIGHT FAIR

* TOTAL COMMITMENT

CONTROLLING FEAR

1. BREATHE

2. STRONG BODY LANGUAGE

3. YELL/ MAKE NOISE

DEFENDING AGAINST FRONTAL ATTACKS

THROAT GRAB

EYE GOUGE

HEEL OF HAND TO NOSE

FIST DOWN ON NOSE

HEAD BUTT

FIST TO GROIN

FINGER PULLS

DEFENDING AGAINST ATTACKS FROM THE REAR

THROAT GRAB

HEAD BUTT

FOOT STOMP

FIST TO GROIN

ELBOW TO GROIN

FINGER PULLS

Chapter 4

WEAPONS

This chapter will deal with two possible situations: what to do if a weapon is used against you, and how you can use weapons against an attacker.

DEFENDING YOURSELF AGAINST WEAPONS

It is always a very personal choice: whether to fight off an attack or try to minimize physical injury by complying with an attacker's demands. My general rule is that if you are facing a **deadly** weapon, you should submit to your attacker's demands. Deadly weapons don't leave a lot of options. Better to come out of this alive than dead! If the attacker is after some material possession alone, there should be no question. **SURVIVAL** is the only important issue!

However, some may believe that they can "take" their attacker. Only you can decide whether, in a particular situation, you should resist an attack. This depends solely on your level of ability and confidence. Even if he has a gun or knife, you may feel that you can disarm and disable him, at least long enough to make your getaway. Or, you may be committed enough to defend your honor to the death. Either way, if you should face an attacker with a weapon, it is imperative that you focus your eyes on the attacker's eyes, and not on the weapon he is using. While this may sound simple enough, you cannot imagine how hypnotizing a gun pointed at your body can be!

Use passive defenses such as gaining sympathy or convincing the attacker to either identify with you as a person, rather than as an object, or find you totally unappealing. Reports from survivors of sexual assault indicate successfully escaping attacks through verbal skills: gaining sympathy by saying they are pregnant, very ill (with herpes or even AIDS), or making themselves very unappealing by vomiting or urinating. **Remember: ANYTHING GOES!**

Let's look at some of the most common weapons used against victims of muggings, sexual attacks, and all other forms of attacks against your person and WHAT YOU CAN DO ABOUT IT!

Gun Attack

GUNS

Most of us are terrified of guns. They are all deadly: revolvers, semi-automatics, assault weapons, hunting rifles. The list goes on and on. Defending yourself against a gun usually involves **TALK**, and the types of passive defenses already discussed. There is no such thing as honesty and fair play in these types of situations.

Believe it or not, if someone is threatening you with a gun, your best defense may be to break and run. First, it is extremely difficult to hit a moving target, particularly when using a handgun. Second, if you are hit, it is very unlikely to be a mortal wound. Finally, the longer you stand and plead or fight with this person, the more likely it is that he will use the gun on you. At the initial confrontation, he is still undecided whether he will use the weapon or not. He is testing your reaction and trying to gather up his courage. As time passes, he may become more committed to injuring you. This is why it is so important not to hesitate, but to act immediately. **RUN!**

If you cannot break away and run, there is a very effective physical defense to use against an attacker who is holding a revolver. A revolver fires bullets through a cylinder, which rotates as the trigger is pulled back. If you face an attacker with a revolver, the first thing to do is turn sideways. This minimizes the size of your body as a target. Take a small step out of the line of fire and distract your attacker with your hands: talk with one hand up high, and the other about waist high. The attacker will usually focus on the higher waving hand. Use the lower hand to grab the gun barrel and cylinder (see opposite page). The gun cannot be fired if the cylinder is held from revolving. Your upper hand should then be used to grab the attacker's throat. This will mean using **deadly** force in striking, grabbing, and squeezing his windpipe. **HE MUST BE SERIOUSLY DISABLED,** at least long enough for you to make your getaway. Disabling him means cutting off his oxygen supply, causing him to choke. As we discussed in the previous chapter, the need for oxygen is so great, that he will probably let go of the gun in his attempt to get your hands off his throat.

Knife Attack

KNIVES

Knives are becoming the weapon of choice on the streets. Everyone seems to carry a knife. They are cheap, and a buyer doesn't need a permit or licence to acquire them. They cause deadly physical damage by either puncturing internal organs or cutting open blood supplies under the skin.

When threatened by someone holding a knife, and passive defenses have not prevented an attack, the only physical defense to a frontal attack is to try to stay out of striking range, and turn sideways (as with a gun). The next step may make you cringe, but you must grab the knife blade with your hand! Yes, it will cut your hand, but there will be far less damage cutting into the palm of your hand than sticking into your heart or spleen! This is particularly important if you are attacked from behind and the knife is being held against your throat. By grasping the blade with your palm, it cannot cut into your throat. (see facing page). You must get it away from your throat. Your other hand should then be reaching for the attacker's throat. **Strike, grab, and squeeze with life and death conviction!**

CLUBS, BATS, STICKS

Clubs, bats, and sticks are generally used by attackers in downward or sideways clubbing motions, most often aimed at the head. If someone is threatening you with this type of weapon, and all of your passive skills have been used up, the most important part of your body to protect is your head. As with all weapons, your best tactic is try to stay out of striking distance. If you cannot escape being struck, try to grab on tight to that weapon, and only let go when you have a clear path to his throat. By grabbing and squeezing his windpipe, he will have to let go of the weapon in order to get your hands off his throat. Hopefully, he will be so busy gasping for air, you will be able to run to safety.

USING WEAPONS TO DEFEND YOURSELF

The most important thing to consider when contemplating purchasing or carrying any kind of weapon for protection is that in the event of an attack, there is always the possibility that your weapon could be taken away from you and used against you. That means, among other things, that an unarmed attack on you could quickly become an armed attack with a weapon which **you** provided. This applies to all types of weapons: guns, knives, pepper sprays, mace, car keys, etc. If you are prepared to use a weapon, you had better use it right the first time, and make sure your attacker cannot take your weapon away from you. Any hesitation could mean your demise.

Another important consideration is that when people are attacked, it is usually so unexpected, and so fast, that they simply do not have time to locate and pull out a weapon. Women most often carry weapons in their purses. There just is not time to open your purse, fumble for a weapon, pull it out, aim it, and use it! Consider the near-fatal dilemma involving one of my colleagues. He was working alone, responding to a complaint of a suspicious person. He located a lone male in an alley. While he was questioning this person, he was extremely cautious, trying to assess this individual's frame of mind. The man was unarmed, but appeared very agitated. Suddenly he leaped on my colleague. As they were wrestling on the ground, the suspect reached for the policeman's gun. The fight was now for possession of the gun, and it was everything the officer could do to keep his gun in his holster. Finally, help arrived, and the suspect was subdued. The policeman was absolutely exhausted from the fight, and when asked how it happened, he could only reply, "It happened so fast, I couldn't draw my gun quickly enough".

The main point here is that this policeman was prepared for a confrontation. He had a gun close to his hand. He is a large, physically fit male, with years of training and experience. And yet, he came very close to having his weapon taken away from him and used on him.

You should not rely solely on a weapon to defend yourself. Chances are you would not have time to pull it out anyway. You have a better chance of survival by practicing physical defenses, and using your highly developed "streetsmarts".

GUNS

Like it or not, I am going to give you my personal opinion of guns. **I HATE GUNS!** I strongly believe in gun control, and that only law enforcement officers should be allowed to carry guns. It makes me ill to think of the hundreds of innocent children killed every year because of the careless storage of guns in the home. However, the reality is that there are a lot of "crazies" out there who have guns, and many law-abiding, sane people, who feel that they need a gun to defend themselves. In fact, over the last few years, the sale of guns to women in the U.S. has increased by 50%. Purchasing a gun is a personal decision, and one which I hope is carefully thought out. The consequences can be deadly.

If you have decided to get a gun, the most important advice that I have for you is to take ongoing instruction on how to use this weapon. You must be so familiar and so comfortable with that gun, that if the time came when you had to use it, you would not hesitate, and you would be sure of hitting your target. This would minimize the chances of it being taken away from you and used against you.

When I started my police recruit training, the only gun I had ever shot was my brothers' air rifle. I was as "gun-shy" as they come. Our trainers spent weeks in the classroom teaching us everything about guns before we actually put our hands on our service revolvers. We were so excited when the day finally arrived when we were to go to the indoor range and actually shoot! Even after all of the instruction and theory we had received, when the time came for me to draw my gun and fire, I was so nervous I almost missed the target! Then came the explosion, the flash from the gunpowder, and the recoil of the gun. It can be quite a shock for someone who hasn't fired a gun before. As part of ongoing police training, we are required to qualify with our handguns several times every year, with a series of surprise targets at different distances. Needless to say, I am now very comfortable with my gun, and in fact, shooting it is second-nature to me. It is part of my uniform, and I don't feel ready to work without it. The point is, this skill and comfort level was only possible with years of training and ongoing qualifying. Two or three lessons by your gun dealer in his indoor range will not give you the level of confidence and competency you will need if the day ever arrives where you have to pull out your gun and use it!

If you are going to acquire a gun, join a gun club after you have received your initial training. Use the gun club as a way of increasing and maintaining your skill level.

KNIVES AND SIMILAR WEAPONS

As mentioned earlier, knives are readily available, inexpensive, and need no permit to be carried. Other stabbing instruments, such as pens, rat-tail combs, keys, etc., are often carried by people, though seldom used as weapons. Again, if you are going to use such weapons, you must be prepared for the fact that they could be taken away from you. Most knives must be taken out of their protective sheaths, and the blade extended before they are ready to be used. As we have discussed, the speed required to use weapons during a surprise attack would make it necessary for you to walk around with these weapons already in your hand.

Make no mistake: knives can be just as deadly as guns. If you are prepared to use one, you must be prepared for the possible deadly consequences. If this is a life-threatening situation requiring deadly force as a defense, do not use it to slash or wound (ie. slashing the arm or leg). Knives are most effective when used in a stabbing motion directed at a vital organ, such as the heart or spleen. If you are not prepared to go that far, or if you hesitate for a fraction of a second, you may lose control of the knife and end up being the one getting stabbed.

MACE, TEAR GAS, AND PEPPER SPRAYS

While some spray products can be very effective weapons, I suggest that before you purchase any, you first check with your local police department. Many are illegal. You may find them in certain gun shops being sold as dog or bear repellants. Some of the downfalls of spray weapons are that some types are awkward to aim, and if used on a windy day, the spray could be carried back into your face. Look for canisters that are designed for ease of grip, so that there will be no fumbling for proper spray direction. Some may be refillable, allowing you to practice on a target. As with all weapons, practice and familiarity are most important. Most police departments now issue pepper sprays to officers as an effective, yet relatively harmless way to stop an attack.

When choosing a pepper spray, check for ease of aiming and firing. Some attach to your keychain, making them immediately accessible when you most need them. Others are carried on the wrist or belt with a velcro strap and small holster, ideal for long walks, jogging, or cycling.

Pepper or Mace Sprays

UMBRELLAS, STICKS, AND JABBING DEVICES

Another weapon police officers carry is the riot or night stick. These come in a variety of lengths and wood types, but usually are made of hard wood, and are approximately 18-21 inches long. Training in the use of these weapons includes, among other things, how to break bones in a striking motion. However, the most effective use of the night stick (or similar device), is jabbing it into the attacker's solar plexus or groin.

Umbrellas, walking sticks, and even a rolled up magazine can be just as effective when this jabbing or stabbing technique is used. The important thing to remember is to hit the solar plexus or groin with enough force to disable your attacker. If you miss your target or don't use enough force, the situation will quickly turn against you. He will be able to grab your weapon, possibly disarm you, and use your weapon against you.

An Umbrella as a Weapon

A Magazine as a Weapon

THE BIG DECISION

The topic of the use of weapons to defend oneself is so important, I feel it necessary here to re-emphasize the pros and cons. Weapons can be great equalizers when it comes to a woman defending herself or her family against someone much larger and stronger than she. It may also give added confidence just knowing it is close by. In "stalking" situations, where a woman is being repeatedly harassed and threatened by an ex-boyfriend or husband, a gun may provide enough peace of mind to enable her to sleep at night. In most cases, an attacker can be wounded, at least to the point where she can make her getaway. If used properly and quickly enough, the woman should be able to escape virtually untouched.

The downside to carrying weapons is the potential danger. At the risk of being repetitive, there is always the chance the weapon can be taken away and used on the innocent victim. In addition, relying on a weapon might give you a false sense of security, or make you take chances, and not use the preventative skills you have learned. Weapons stored in the house often cause accidental injury or death to innocent loved ones. And finally, the decision to actually use a deadly weapon on another human being is an extremely difficult one. You must be prepared to live with the consequences.

You should now be able to make an informed decision about carrying and using weapons. If you decide to utilize one of these weapons, do not forget the importance of prevention and practicing all of the physical defenses as well. Chances are, in an sudden attack, these will be the only defenses available to you!

KEY POINTS TO REMEMBER

PHYSICAL DEFENSES VS: *GUNS*   * BREAK and RUN (if possible)

                                                  * TURN SIDEWAYS

                                                  * GRAB THE CYLINDER

                                                  * GO FOR THE THROAT

                       KNIVES   * BREAK and RUN (if possible)

                                                  * STAY OUT OF STRIKING
                                                     RANGE

                                                  * TURN SIDEWAYS

                                                  * GRAB THE BLADE

                                                  * GO FOR THE THROAT

            CLUBS, BATS, STICKS   * BREAK and RUN (if possible)

                                                  * STAY OUT OF STRIKING
                                                     RANGE

                                                  * PROTECT YOUR HEAD

                                                  * GRAB THE WEAPON

                                                  * GO FOR THE THROAT

USING WEAPONS TO DEFEND YOURSELF:

            * SURVIVAL IS THE ONLY CONSIDERATION

            * TOTAL COMMITMENT

            * BE PREPARED FOR DEADLY CONSEQUENCE

            * YOUR WEAPON CAN BE USED AGAINST YOU

THE AFTERMATH

If the unspeakable happens: you are victimized in a personal, physical assault, you must then decide on a course of action, including who you will tell. Often, this extremely important decision is made when a survivor is physically and mentally traumatized. While criminal investigations and the gathering of evidence are best conducted immediately following an offense, this is also the worst possible time for a victim to make good decisions.

Survivors of any violent crime appear to suffer similar aftereffects: anger, denial, fear, vulnerability, guilt, shame, loss of self-esteem, paranoia, depression, and on and on. Interestingly, it does not seem to matter if the attacker is a total stranger, or is well known to the victim. In other words, these same aftereffects are suffered by someone who is attacked by a family member or acquaintance, in the woman's own home, as by a complete stranger lurking in the bushes.

One woman I know of had been in a jewellery store with her two small children when the store was robbed. She and the kids were made to lay on the floor by two gun-welding thugs. While her contact with the robbers was minimal, this woman sought help in dealing with her feelings of vulnerability shortly after the incident. She felt the need to make her home more secure, would not let her children out of her sight, and she suffered nightly insomnia. These feelings continued, even after the robbers were caught. Fortunately, help was there for her. She and the children were given therapy sessions with trauma counsellors and others who had been in similar situations. All three are doing fine now. Most importantly, she recognized that she needed help in dealing with these very natural emotions, and she was made aware that this help was readily available to her. Victim advocate programs are growing in strength and numbers. To the best of my knowledge, every major police department in North America has some type of victim assistance program in place. There are many valuable resources only a phone call away.

Statistics show that only one in ten sexual assaults are ever reported to the police. Sexual assault center workers tell me that while they are getting more and more calls every day from women, children, and men in need of assistance, many do not want to enter into the legal process, but are overcome by the need to tell someone. Some have tried for years to forget what has happened to them, but have found that the emotions keep surfacing. This affects every aspect of their lives. Dealing with the trauma of violent crime is an extremely important issue and it must be handled by trained counsellors or professional therapists. The decision whether to report the attack to police should always be left up to the survivor.

Those who do seek help from the police are usually motivated by a desire to see their attacker caught and punished. Others recognize the importance of stopping criminals from continuing to victimize others. The next target could be their sister or mother. Criminals never attack only once. They offend repeatedly, usually with increasing violence, until finally, they are caught and imprisoned. While it is never pleasant going through the judicial process, it is the only civilized way to stop these violent offenders. The following is an explanation of some of the events and consequences the survivor of a serious assault could expect to encounter from the police, the justice system, and the community.

THE ROLE OF THE POLICE

Most police departments have highly trained investigators for specific types of crimes. They are specialized in particular areas: child abuse, sex crimes, robbery, to name a few. This also means that they have other professionals available to them as resources: interpreters, crisis teams, sexual assault counsellors, and so on. Most investigators are trained to be highly sensitive to the victim's traumatized state. More and more female officers are being added to investigation teams which require a woman's sensitivity.

The primary job of a police investigator is to gather evidence. This means determining, first of all, if a crime has been committed, getting a description of the offender, locating the offender, and collecting all of the evidence needed to link this individual to committing the crime. After a victim calls for help from the police, attending officers will determine what type of crime has been committed. In cases of physical attacks, victims are taken to the hospital for a medical assessment. Evidence is gathered by doctors and nurses who are trained in detecting the types of evidence needed for connecting a suspect to the crime: body fluids, hair samples, etc. Before the assault survivor is taken to the hospital, crisis workers or sexual assault counsellors are normally contacted to meet at the hospital. They will stay with the survivor throughout her physical examination, and will then arrange follow-up services for her. From here, she is taken to a safe place, usually her home, where a written statement may be taken. This will help to refresh her memory if she must testify in court some time in the future. Often, she will remember more details after the initial shock and trauma has passed. It may appear to many crime victims that police officers are impersonal and don't seem to care. Investigators cannot become personally involved in a case. While, being sensitive to the survivor's circumstance, they must maintain their objectivity at all costs. An interesting story should help to illustrate this point:

I once attended a seminar on detecting signs of child abuse. The lecturer was a world-renowned expert in this area. Several years earlier, he had investigated a case of incest, where a very young child had been repeatedly raped by her step-father. The case did not come to trial for over a year, and during that time, the detective had developed protective, deeply caring emotions toward the little girl. When the case finally came to trial, the detective was giving his expert opinion as to how the injuries on the child must have occurred. He spoke with such contempt in his voice, all the time looking at the step-father, that the judge finally cut him off. The judge stated that it was so obvious that the detective despised the accused, that he could not possibly give an impartial report to the court. The case was dismissed, and the accused walked out of court a free man. This was the cost of becoming emotionally involved!

THE JUSTICE SYSTEM

This is an area of serious concern to most of us. We have seen a steady erosion of the rights of crime victims and honest citizens, while the rights of those accused of committing crimes have been increasingly protected. There appears to be no serious consequences for those committing the crimes. Our courts are over-crowded and backlogged. Trials are often delayed for a year or more after the offense occurs. Witnesses and victims of crimes become frustrated with the process and often forget details which are crucial to the case. Some feel re-victimized after being cross-examined by an aggressive defense attorney. Sentences are seen as far too lenient. Offenders are released on parole after serving a fraction of their sentence.

But for all of its weaknesses, our judicial system appears to be slowly changing for the better. Victim advocate groups, citizen action committees, and police associations are all demanding changes to the system. I believe that we will see more help in the future for crime victims, and harsher penalties for convicted criminals. But these changes are only possible if we all work within the system. Witnesses and victims of crime must step forward and be heard. If we pretend we did not see something, or fail to report an offense because of lack of faith in the justice system, then we will never affect changes to the system. We will, in fact, be part of the failure of the system.

SOCIETY

There is no doubt: we are living in an increasingly violent society. These are also times of great economic uncertainty. History has shown that there is a direct correlation between economic slumps and crimes of violence. Women and children will always be the most common targets of these types of crimes. We have come a long way, in that more and more victims are stepping forward to be heard. However, we still have a long, long way to go to end the violence. Unless the movie, T.V., and print industries stop promoting violence and pornography, we are surely headed for more and more violence in our daily lives. Just watch the evening news if you have any doubts.

While we don't want to be paranoid and afraid to trust anyone, we should all be aware of potentially dangerous situations. Using the preventative techniques discussed earlier in this book will reduce your chances of becoming a target for criminals. However, with crime rates on the rise, the odds are that you will one day become the victim of some type of violent crime.

It is very hard for anyone to admit that they are vulnerable. Crime victims often feel that they have lost control or power over their lives. They feel unsafe in their own community. Reporting crimes and following them through the investigative and judicial processes allows the closure necessary for the survivor to regain some of this control, and to start over.

We all have a responsibility to the rest of our society to try to make it a better place for future generations. This is only possible if we help one another stand up to the "bullies" of the world. We must support and encourage others to not only fight back, but report all offenses to the authorities. We owe it to the others in our society who might become targets of similar violent attacks.

CONCLUSION

The main objective of this book has been to raise your level of awareness and change your attitude. Being aware of the potential dangers to you and your loved ones will help you to avoid and prevent them from happening to you. Use the preventative methods we have discussed and you will greatly reduce your chances of becoming a target. Be prepared for any situation, and have a plan. Mental and physical preparedness comes with practice. Role playing and mental imaging will be the best methods of preparing yourself for violent situations.

Attitude is a difficult thing to change. You may not be very confident or strong in your professional or personal life. It can also be very difficult for some to reach the level of anger and aggression needed to successfully do battle with someone who is much bigger and stronger. You may not be a very physical person. Not everyone has made fitness a big part of their lives. Or, you may have health problems or physical handicaps which restrict your activities. The single most important goal for you should be to protect yourself from physical harm. This can be done by running away, talking your way out, or fighting to escape. There is no honorable or brave way out of these situations. SURVIVAL IS ALL THAT IS IMPORTANT!

Only you can decide in a life and death situation which defense is best for you. If a physical defense is chosen, act fast and aggressively. Do not hesitate. Show no mercy. The basic survival techniques which you have learned are not for "fair fights". Always assume that an aggressor is dangerous, and do not underestimate his capabilities.

Report all incidents to the police, no matter how trivial you think they are. Others cannot be warned of potential dangers if the police don't know there is a problem developing. Wouldn't you want to know if there was a rash of house breakings or car thefts in your neighborhood? What about a "flasher" or a child molester? Of course you want to know about all crimes in your community.

If you have been attacked, DO NOT BLAME YOURSELF! You did not bring on this attack- HE DID. Tell someone about it. Help is out there. You cannot forget it or pretend it did not happen. Join or start your own support group. There are many excellent groups which help survivors get through this experience. Contact can be made through any of the victim advocate associations or your local sexual assault center. Help is out there. You need only ask for it.

In an effort to end the violence in our society, we must help each other by preventing more violent attacks. The only way to stop an attacker from hurting others is to report the crime to the police, and follow through with charges to a conclusion in court.

Finally, it is time for all of us to stand up and yell...

WE HAVE THE RIGHT TO SAY NO!

WE WILL DO WHATEVER IT TAKES TO DEFEND OURSELVES!

WE WILL STOP YOU FROM HURTING OTHERS!

WE'RE FIGHTING BACK!

REFERENCES

BARTHOL,Robert G.(1979). "PROTECT YORSELF".Prentice-Hall Inc., Englewood Cliffs, N.J.

BENEDICT, Helen (1987). "SAFE, STRONG, & STREETWISE".Little, Brown,and Company, Toronto.

CAIGNON, Denise and GROVES,Gail (1987)."HER WITS ABOUT HER". Harper & Row, New York.

FEIN,Judith (1988). "ARE YOU A TARGET?".Torrance Publishing Company, Duncan Mills, Ca.

GOODMAN,Fay(1988). "SELF DEFENCE FOR ALL". A&C Black Limited, London.

McCALLUM,Paul(1991). "A PRACTICAL SELF-DEFENCE GUIDE FOR WOMEN". Betterway Publications Inc., White Hall, Virginia.

MCGURN, Thomas (1984)."THE WOMAN'S BIBLE FOR SURVIVAL IN A VIOLENT SOCIETY". Stein and Day Publishers, New York.

MERCER, Shirley Litch (188). "NOT A PRETTY PICTURE: AN EXPLORATORY STUDY OF VIOLENCE AGAINST WOMEN IN HIGH SCHOOL DATING RELATIONSHIPS". Toronto

PETERSON, Susan G.(1979). "SELF-DEFENSE FOR WOMEN THE WESTPOINT WAY". Simon and Schuster, New York.

WHITELAW, Judd (1985). "PROTECT YOURSELF: EVERY WOMAN'S SURVIVAL COURSE". Blandford Press, Poole, Dorset:Sterling Publishing Co., New York.

ORDER FORM

Send copies of this book to someone you care about: mother, grandmother, aunt, sister, daughter, niece, friend! Everyone should know these life-saving techniques. Mail this completed form, along with a check or money order to:

> Beauvoir
> P.O. Box 64257
> 5512 4 St. N.W.
> Calgary, Ab. T2K 6J1
> Canada

Please Send _____ copies of "Fighting Back" to:

Name: _____

Address: _____

_____

City: _____

Prov./State: _____

Postal / Zip Code: _____

Enclosed is my check or money order as follows:

___ books at **$9.95** each = _____
      *No G.S.T.

Shipping rate of $3.00 for the first book and $1.50 for each additional book shipped at the same time (U.S. orders $4.00 and $2.00) = _____

Total Amount Enclosed = _____

Orders must be pre-paid: no C.O.D.'s